AXIS PARENT GUIDES SERIES

A Parent's Guide to the Sex Talk

A Parent's Guide to Pornography

A Parent's Guide to Sexual Assault

A Parent's Guide to Suicide & Self-Harm
Prevention

A Parent's Guide to Depression & Anxiety

A Parent's Guide to Tough Conversations

A Parent's Guide to Cancel Culture

A Parent's Guide to Racism in the United States

A Parent's Guide to Walking through Grief

A Parent's Guide to Talking about Death

PARENT GUIDE BUNDLES

Parent Guides to Social Media

Parent Guides to Finding True Identity

Parent Guides to Mental & Sexual Health

Parent Guides to Connecting in Chaos

A PARENT'S GUIDE TO CANCEL CULTURE

A PARENT'S GUIDE TO

CANCEL CULTURE

Tyndale House Publishers
Carol Stream, Illinois

Visit Tyndale online at tyndale.com.

Visit Axis online at axis.org.

Tyndale and Tyndale's quill logo are registered trademarks of Tyndale House Ministries.

A Parent's Guide to Cancel Culture

For information about special discounts for bulk purchases, please contact Tyndale House Publishers at csresponse@tyndale.com, or call 1-855-277-8400.

Library of Congress Cataloging-in-Publication Data

A catalog record for this book is available from the Library of Congress.

ISBN 978-1-4964-6778-2

Printed in the United States of America

29 28 27 26 25 24 23
7   6   5   4   3   2   1

You can do something stupid when you're 15, say one thing and 10 years later that shapes how people perceive you. We all do cringey things and make dumb mistakes and whatever. But social media's existence has brought that into a place where people can take something you did back then and make it who you are now.

L., AGE 16,
IN AN INTERVIEW WITH THE
NEW YORK TIMES

CONTENTS

A LETTER FROM AXIS

Dear Reader,

We're Axis, and since 2007, we've been creating resources to help connect parents, teens, and Jesus in a disconnected world. We're a group of gospel-minded researchers, speakers, and content creators, and we're excited to bring you the best of what we've learned about making meaningful connections with the teens in your life.

This parent's guide is designed to help start a conversation. Our goal is to give you enough knowledge that you're able to ask your teen informed questions about their world. For each guide, we spend weeks reading, researching, and interviewing parents and teens in order to distill everything you need to know about the topic at hand. We encourage you to read the whole thing and then to use the questions we include to get the conversation going with your teen—and then to follow the conversation wherever it leads.

As Douglas Stone, Bruce Patton, and Sheila Heen point out in their book *Difficult Conversations*, "Changes in attitudes and behavior rarely come about because of arguments, facts, and attempts to persuade. How often do *you* change your values and beliefs—or whom you love or what you want in life—based on something someone tells you? And how likely are you to do so when the person who is trying to change you doesn't seem fully aware of the reasons you see things differently in the first place?"[1] For whatever reason, when we believe that others are trying to understand *our* point of view, our defenses usually go down, and we're more willing to listen to *their* point of view. The rising generation is no exception.

So we encourage you to ask questions, to listen, and then to share your heart with your teen. As we often say at Axis, discipleship happens where conversation happens.

Sincerely,
Your friends at Axis

---

[1] Douglas Stone, Bruce Patton, and Sheila Heen, *Difficult Conversations: How to Discuss What Matters Most*, rev. ed. (New York: Penguin Books, 2010), 137.

YOU'RE
CANCELED

People tend to see cancellation as either wholly good—there are new consequences for saying or doing racist, bigoted or otherwise untenable things—or wholly bad, in that people can lose their reputations and in some cases their jobs, all because a mob has taken undue offense to a clumsy or out-of-context remark. Personally, I think it's best viewed not as either positive or negative, but as something else: a new development in the way that power works—a development brought about by social media.

JONAH E. BROMWICH[1]

WHAT IF THE WORST THING you'd ever done was filmed and then shared with millions of people online? What if thousands of strangers judged you based on that snippet of your life? In a time when smartphones can instantly broadcast our worst sins to the world, and when digging through someone's online dirt is as easy as typing a few keywords, the internet can be a strange and frightening place. This is the era of cancel culture, which generally refers to calling people out on social media to suffer punitive consequences for inappropriate behavior or speech. And it's got many people wondering, *"Is cancel culture a mob mentality, or a long overdue way of speaking truth to power?"*[2]

Cancel culture generally refers to calling people out on social media to suffer punitive consequences for inappropriate behavior or speech.

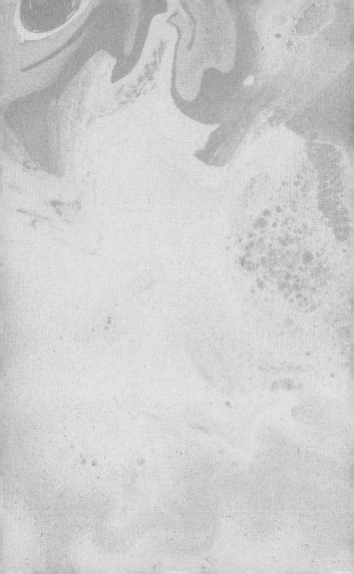

#FIREAMYCOOPER

"SHE LOST HER JOB, HER HOME, and her public life. Now some demand her freedom? How many lives are we going to destroy over misunderstood 60-second videos on social media?"

That statement was made by Amy Cooper's lawyer, Robert Barnes. You're probably familiar with the viral video where Ms. Cooper hysterically called a 911 operator after Christian Cooper (unrelated) calmly asked her to leash her dog. She said, "I'm in the Ramble, there is a man, African American, he has a bicycle helmet, and he is recording me and threatening me and my dog."[3] She clarified over and over that this African American man was threatening her, invoking the stereotype that because he was Black, she was in real danger.

The video sparked well-deserved outrage that racial prejudice was so shamelessly exploited. Christian Cooper did nothing wrong, yet Amy's call to the police weaponized his Blackness as she pretended to be at risk.

But how to respond? What does Amy Cooper deserve? How would we want to be treated if one of the worst things we'd done was broadcast for the world to see?

The next day she was fired. She publicly apologized, yet people continued to call for her head. Eventually, even Mr. Cooper said in an interview, "I'm uncomfortable with defining someone by a couple of seconds of what they've done. No excusing that it was a racist act. But does that define her entire life?"[4]

To what extent should someone be made to pay for their past?

Many of us echo his question, a query about the effectiveness of cancel culture: To what extent should someone be made to pay for their past? How do we determine what is appropriate to say and do? Should justice primarily be about punishment? How can we hold people, especially powerful and influential people, accountable?

WHAT DOES IT MEAN TO BE CANCELED?

GETTING CANCELED can look like online shaming, losing followers, getting fired, being encouraged to apologize, or even receiving death threats.

There's a long list of people (and companies) who have been canceled over the years: Bill O'Reilly, Madison Beer, Kim Kardashian, Ellen DeGeneres, Kanye West, John Crist, Jordan Peterson, Equinox Fitness, J. K. Rowling, James Charles, Scarlett Johansson, Louis C.K., Netflix . . . and they were all canceled for different reasons (sexual abuse scandals, insensitive comments, racist acts, political ideologies).[5] Sometimes cancellation lasts a few weeks. Sometimes it's permanent.

Getting canceled isn't just for celebrities. The *New York Times* interviewed teens around the country to understand what the term means to Gen Z.

Alex is seventeen, and she hears the word *canceled* every day at her high school outside Atlanta. It can be a joke, but it can also suggest that an offending person won't be tolerated again. Alex thinks of it as a permanent label. "Now they'll forever be thought of as that action, not for the person they are," she said.[6]

Some see cancel culture as necessary accountability, a way to make people take responsibility for the harm they've caused. Others argue that it's a means of censorship. In the US, cancel culture is politicized (by the left and the right), controversial, and emotionally fraught. Its existence highlights how hard it is to relate well with other humans, especially the humans we don't understand or agree with.

Cancel culture's existence
highlights how hard
it is to relate well with
other humans, especially
the humans we don't
understand or agree with.

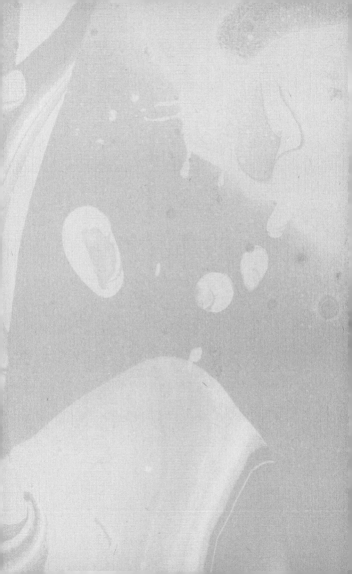

HOW DID WE
GET HERE?

- In the 1991 film *New Jack City*, Wesley Snipes's character Nino Brown says about his girlfriend, "Cancel that b****, I'll buy another one." It's probably the first time that the term "canceled" was used for a person, not a credit card.[7]

- By 2015, "You're canceled" became a way to express both serious and joking disapproval on Black Twitter. Over time, the phrase was used to call celebrities and organizations to account.

- Although many people still use the terms "cancel culture" and "callout culture" interchangeably, some argue that they have become distinct movements. Callout culture uses social media to point out a problem; cancel culture goes further, advocating for real-life consequences, calling for the job, fame, or reputation of the accused offender.

- Then, with the global pandemic and lockdown, it seemed like someone new was getting canceled every other week, or trying to cancel someone in response to being canceled (and if you're confused, don't worry, everyone is confused).

- Michael Barbaro explains, "As the world moves even more online during the pandemic, greater attention and weight is being given to the things that happen there."[8] Complex, nuanced opinions held by multifaceted, embodied people are exchanged on platforms that reward certainty, simplicity, and outrage. Rather than seeing the

Callout culture uses social media to point out a problem; cancel culture goes further, advocating for real-life consequences, calling for the job, fame, or reputation of the accused offender.

person on the other end of the discussion as a complete human being with insecurities and idiosyncrasies, they are reduced to a defeatable party who must be proven wrong. This has always been a hazard of social media, but heightened emotional rawness from the isolation, stress, and uncertainty of the pandemic made the stakes feel higher and the frenzy more palpable.

- So here we are, in what feels like a more polarized environment than ever, trying to decide what is appropriate to say and do, and what consequences people should face when they cross the lines that we draw.

WHAT'S THE GOAL OF CANCEL CULTURE?

CANCEL CULTURE ATTEMPTS to correct the long-standing problem that with enough wealth, scandals disappear, victims stay quiet, and abuse continues. The #MeToo movement highlighted how common-place sexual harassment is, and how rarely perpetrators are prosecuted. Cancel culture's goal of holding people—especially powerful and influential people—account-able is well-intentioned. If the law doesn't bring about justice, public scrutiny can still make things happen.

Anne Charity Hudley, associate dean of educational affairs and professor of education at Stanford University, explains why cancel culture is an important tool for minorities:

> If you don't have the ability to
> stop something through political
> means, what you can do is refuse to

participate. . . . Canceling is a way to acknowledge that you don't have to have the power to change structural inequality. . . . But as an individual, you can still have power beyond measure. When you see people canceling Kanye, canceling other people, it's a collective way of saying, "We elevated your social status, your economic prowess, [and] we're not going to pay attention to you in the way that we once did. . . . "I may have no power, but the power I have is to [ignore] you."[9]

Cancel culture affirms that ideas have consequences. Ideologies don't stay in ivory towers. They get walked out, to the benefit or detriment of individuals and society. So the words we use and the policies we promote do matter, and we are responsible for the ideas and actions we put out in the world.

The words we use and the policies we promote do matter, and we are responsible for the ideas and actions we put out in the world.

WHAT'S CONCERNING ABOUT CANCEL CULTURE?

BUT HERE'S THE CATCH: When we call for someone to be canceled, what are we accomplishing? Does canceling someone provide true justice? As mentioned earlier, it's hard to make sweeping statements about cancel culture because so many people have been canceled for very different offenses (Bill O'Reilly's firing based on sexual harassment charges is different from Kanye getting canceled for saying that slavery was a choice, which is different from Alison Roman's *New York Times* column being put on hold after she slighted Chrissy Teigen). Cancel culture seems to say, "If you do something wrong, you're supposed to be out of here. And it could have been five minutes ago, or it could have been 20, 30 years ago."[10] It seems that the same level of severity (*We won't listen to you anymore. You should be publicly disgraced. You should lose your job.*) is applied to every cancellation, without a way to determine proportionate responses.

This is one reason why cancel culture concerns many people. Over 150 influential experts in a variety of fields signed "A Letter on Justice and Open Debate," published in *Harper's Magazine*, essentially protesting cancel culture:

> The free exchange of information and ideas, the lifeblood of a liberal society, is daily becoming more constricted. . . . [We're seeing] an intolerance of opposing views, a vogue for public shaming and ostracism, and the tendency to dissolve complex policy issues in a blinding moral certainty. We uphold the value of robust and even caustic counter-speech from all quarters. But it is now all too

common to hear calls for swift
and severe retribution in response
to perceived transgressions of
speech and thought. . . .

Editors are fired for running
controversial pieces; . . . journalists
are barred from writing on
certain topics; . . . and the heads
of organizations are ousted
for what are sometimes just
clumsy mistakes. Whatever the
arguments around each particular
incident, the result has been to
steadily narrow the boundaries
of what can be said without
the threat of reprisal. . . . The
restriction of debate, whether
by a repressive government or
an intolerant society, invariably
hurts those who lack power and
makes everyone less capable of
democratic participation. The way

to defeat bad ideas is by exposure, argument, and persuasion, not by trying to silence or wish them away.[11]

The letter highlights several concerns about cancel culture. We've already mentioned a few of them, including disproportionate consequences (getting fired, for instance), reductionism (unfair blanket judgments based on a single poor decision), and mob mentality, but here are a few more to discuss with your teen:

No redemption: According to attorney Jill K. Sanders, "Cancel culture flies in the face of restorative justice. Rather than having a conversation about how to restore those involved in criminal acts, perpetrators are just cancelled. There is no path to healing, to learning, or to making things right. Cancel culture is, in

Cancel culture flies in the face of restorative justice. Rather than having a conversation about how to restore those involved in criminal acts, perpetrators are just canceled.

—ATTORNEY JILL K. SANDERS

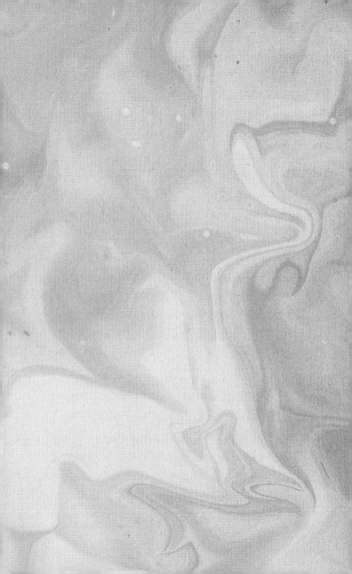

essence, very carceral in that perpetrators are merely punished, and are not given an opportunity to make amends or address the underlying issues which resulted in their behaviors."[12]

Encouragement to hide: For a while, a well-known mission organization had a "three strikes, you're out" policy for porn use, with the good intention of requiring its leaders to be above reproach. But the policy had unintended consequences. Because missionaries were afraid of losing their jobs, some of them hid their porn addictions and never got help. This policy came from the same mindset that fuels cancel culture. If someone messes up, according to the policy, they should be permanently removed from leadership. One mistake defines someone's "goodness" or "badness" forever. If a person knows that past mistakes will write the final conclusion to their story (and that apologizing really won't help), the only sane response is to hide their failure.

Questionable motives: Sean D. Young, executive director of the University of California Institute for Prediction Technology, asks an important question about what motivates people to dig through celebrities' pasts to expose previous insensitivity: "At what point are you doing it to bring awareness [to bigotry] and try to bring some positive impact and try to prevent it from being done again and at what point is it just bullying?"[13]

No lasting change: Canceling celebrities feels powerful, but for the most part it doesn't have long-lasting results. Jack S., a Twitter user who was part of the movement to cancel Lana Del Rey, acknowledges: "She's going to be forgiven because that's always what happens when a celebrity is canceled. It trends over the course of a few days . . . and their fans will continue to like them as if nothing happened."[14] We have to ask ourselves, *Is this the best use of our energy?*

Disagreement silenced: There's been heated discussion about the role of free speech on university campuses for a while now. We're not going to pretend to have a satisfactory answer to that conundrum in this parent's guide, but we realize that cancel culture, safe spaces, and free speech are interrelated. Here's the issue: words hurt. One response has been to create safe spaces, places where offensive ideas aren't tolerated so that students don't have to worry about being triggered and re-traumatized. Whoever said the offensive thing is canceled on a micro-scale as a way of holding them responsible for their harmful words.

But do these compassionate measures help or hurt Gen Z? Greg Lukianoff and Jonathan Haidt write about what they call "the untruth of fragility" in their book *The Coddling of the American Mind*:

> The culture of safetyism is based on a fundamental misunderstanding of human nature and of the dynamics of trauma and recovery. It is vital that people who have survived violence become habituated to ordinary cues and reminders woven into the fabric of daily life. Avoiding triggers is a symptom of PTSD, not a treatment for it.[15]

It's a scary and messy proposition, but what if we all talked regularly with someone we deeply disagreed with about topics we hold close to our hearts?

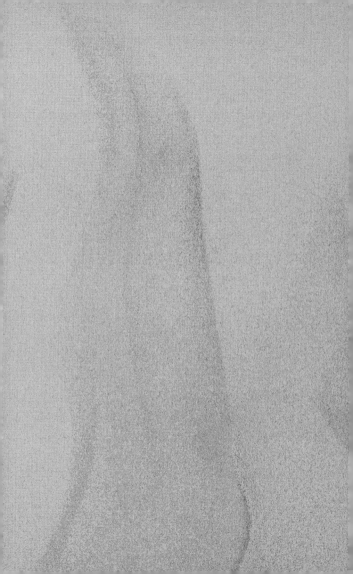

Human beings are what he and other psychologists call "antifragile." Without difficulty, we don't grow. We're more than just resilient (able to endure hardship). We actually need challenges to improve. This is true for our bodies (exercise, literally tearing and stretching our muscles, makes us stronger) and our minds (respectful debate helps us clarify what we believe and allows us to discover truth).

Professor Geoffrey Stone explains why the University of Chicago promotes free speech so fiercely: "The proper response to ideas [students] find offensive, unwarranted and dangerous is not interference, obstruction, or suppression. It is, instead, to engage in robust counterspeech that challenges the merits of those ideas and exposes them for what they are."[16] Cancel culture fosters the opposite environment, where if you say something offensive about a sacred topic—usually race or sexual orientation—at the very least you're uninvited from public discourse. While the motives are often good, the result is an echo chamber where dissent is banned because challenge is seen as dangerous.

Ostracism: A friend of ours attends weekly flat-earther meetings. He's a globe-head (i.e., he believes the earth is round), so why hang out with a group that most of us would call crazy and con-spiratorial? Well, open, kind conversations can help people change their minds.[17] Daryl Davis, a Black man who attends KKK rallies, found the same thing to be true. In his TED Talk, he explains how he became friends with an imperial wizard of the Ku Klux Klan:

I thought, *You know what? Who better to ask, "How can you hate me when you don't even know me?" than someone who would join an organization whose historical premise has been hating those who do not look like them and who do not believe as they believe?* . . . And we conversed—agreed on some things, disagreed on other things. . . . I wasn't there to fight him; I was there to learn from him: where does this ideology come from? Because once you learn where it comes from, you can then try to figure out how to address it and see where it's going.[18]

That imperial wizard is no longer a member of the Klan, all because Mr. Davis befriended him and heard him out. Rally after rally. Year after year. Our friend and Mr. Davis asked themselves, *How can we meet people where they are?* Flat-earthers are mostly greeted with pity, and radical Klansmen with disdain. What's more, they seem to deserve that pity and disdain. Yet when we push people to the edges of society and don't welcome their disagreement, they are left with no place to go but increasingly radical, narrow, self-confirming echo chambers.

It's a scary and messy proposition, but what if we all talked regularly with someone we deeply disagreed with about topics we hold close to our hearts? What if we really listened to each other? What if we were willing to be wrong? What if we were bold enough to have a conversation when we disagreed?

BIBLICAL PRINCIPLES TO HELP US NAVIGATE CANCEL CULTURE

TRUTH EXISTS. Cancel culture affirms that some viewpoints are correct and others are incorrect, that some things are true and others untrue. It points to a deep desire for justice and the protection of marginalized people.

All truth is God's truth. God set the boundaries of reality in place. Whenever we bump up against truth, we are bumping up against the way God made the world. This means we can acknowledge that someone we generally disagree with may believe certain true things. Atheists and Buddhists and secularists and Muslims, for example, espouse both true and false ideas. So do people who have been canceled. Follow in the footsteps of the Bereans and question every idea, asking God what merit a source has and what it gets wrong (see Acts 17:11).

Shame doesn't lead to lasting change.
Cancel culture utilizes shame, saying you
didn't just do a bad thing; you *are* bad.
As Dan Allender puts it, "No one escapes
the assault of a sneer, a disdainful roll
of the eyes. Shame pierces as we feel
belittled and exposed as foolish, weak, or
undesirable."[19] Think about the last time
someone changed your mind about
something. How did they convince you
that you were wrong? By scoffing at
you? By putting you down? By flaunting
your failure? Probably not. Those tactics
rarely work. Paul writes in Romans that
God's kindness leads us to repentance
(see Romans 2:4). Let's consider what
we need in moments of exposure and
offer that to those around us.

Without grace, failure is crushing. We
hate messing up. Yet failure is important.
It's how we learn. In her book *Mindset*,

The only reason we can boldly look our sin in the face, plumbing the depths of our own inadequacy, is because God's loving gaze does not turn away from even the ugliest parts of us.

Carol Dweck differentiates between growth mindset and fixed mindset.[20] Growth mindset recognizes that everyone is in process, that it's always possible to improve with time and effort. People with a growth mindset aren't afraid of failing because they realize good habits don't always come naturally or easily. Fixed mindset, a driving force of cancel culture, says talent and ability are innate and unchangeable, so hide your mistakes if you want approval and admiration.

Christianity tells a paradoxical story about human identity. We think Aleksandr Solzhenitsyn sums it up best: "The line dividing good and evil cuts through the heart of every human being."[21] We are all broken. We all fail. Miserably. Yet we are all made in the image of an astounding God, giving each of us inestimable value.

The only reason we can boldly look our sin in the face, plumbing the depths of our own inadequacy, is because God's loving gaze does not turn away from even the ugliest parts of us. God invites us to stop hiding, to evaluate ourselves honestly so that we can enjoy ever more freedom from our broken mindsets and behaviors. Jesus' righteousness covers our failure (see 2 Corinthians 5:21). His obedience on our behalf is the surest foundation for a growth mindset. Our value is permanently secure because Jesus lived perfectly when we could not. We have nothing left to earn, nothing left to prove. Henri Nouwen says it this way:

> Every time you feel hurt, offended, or rejected, you have to dare to say to yourself: "These feelings, strong as they may be, are not telling me the truth about myself.

The truth, even though I cannot feel it right now, is that I am the chosen child of God, precious in God's eyes, called the Beloved from all eternity, and held safe in an everlasting embrace."[22]

Confession brings healing. "Confess your sins to one another and pray for one another, that you may be healed" (James 5:16, ESV). Because of Jesus' work on our behalf, we get to fully and freely admit how often we say and do dumb things. None of us has arrived. We all slip up because we're all sinful, in need of grace. This reality gives us the freedom to bring our failure into the light. Remember, we're all still figuring things out, and we need help from the Holy Spirit and our community to overcome sin. Is cancel culture providing space for us to confess and get help?

Nuance is difficult but essential. Simplicity rarely loses to complexity on social media. Maybe this is why online dialogue feels increasingly pointless and fraught. Twitter and other social media platforms reward absolutes instead of nuance. Conviction over questions. Certainty over openness. There is no space for "umm" or "I haven't figured that out yet." James 1:19-20 instructs believers to be "quick to listen, slow to speak and slow to become angry" (NIV). Our revolutionary calling is to think slowly, to critically evaluate our own opinions, and to acknowledge when we're wrong.

Humility is key. What if we entered discussions asking, "What can I learn from you?" instead of "How can I prove you wrong?" We should be thankful for correction. It would be incredibly arrogant to think that we have every issue completely

Jesus was not afraid to engage with disreputable people, even though He lost social credibility by spending time with outcasts. Let's follow His example.

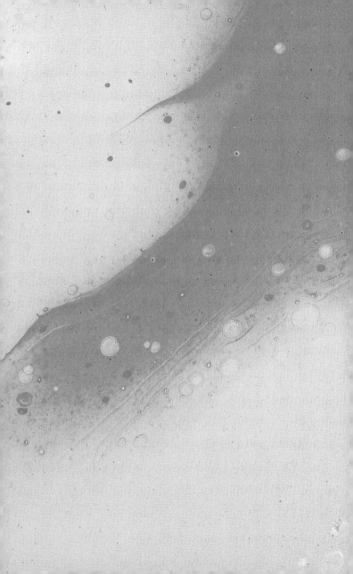

figured out. Because we believe we are in process, still being renewed day by day, we should be grateful for opportunities where weakness is exposed and rooted out.

We don't have to be defensive. Jesus was not afraid to engage with disreputable people, even though He lost social credibility by spending time with outcasts. Let's follow His example and stop worrying about whether associating with someone will damage our reputation. What would it look like to befriend those who've been pushed to the margins? To care about both "cancelers" and those who have been canceled?

Give people the benefit of the doubt. Unless you have reason to believe otherwise, assume that someone has good motives even when they say something offensive. If, upon further investigation, you learn they were trying to be inflammatory, that's a different discussion. But a lot of the time people say careless things unintentionally, and they simply need someone to tell them why their words were hurtful. This provides an opportunity to move forward in a productive way rather than cancel the other person outright.

FINAL THOUGHTS

Let he who is without sin among
you cast the first stone at her.

JESUS

This idea of purity and you're never compromised and you're always politically woke and all that stuff—you should get over that quickly. The world is messy. There are ambiguities. People who do really good stuff have flaws. People who you are fighting may love their kids. . . . One danger I see among young people, particularly on college campuses . . . there is this sense sometimes of, "The way of me making change is to be as judgmental as possible about other people." . . . That's not activism. That's not bringing about change. If all you're doing is casting stones, you're probably not going to get that far.

FORMER PRESIDENT BARACK OBAMA

IF ONLY THERE WERE "bad people" and "good people." Wouldn't that make so many issues simpler? We could round up all the awful folks and live in a peaceful world. But if you haven't noticed, each one of us has a profound capacity to hurt and a profound ability to heal. Every day we make choices—some helping ourselves and others, some causing angst to ourselves and those around us. The world is messy. We are messy. And it shouldn't surprise us to find brokenness in others and dysfunction in ourselves. This is ultimately why Jesus came, because we can't fix ourselves, and without His help, we just keep wounding others no matter how hard we try not to. So as we consider the most embarrassing things we've said, or the worst things we've done, let's also consider how we want to be heard and treated in the midst of our failings. Jesus came to redeem and transform all of us,

Jesus came to redeem and transform all of us, including those who have made racist, sexist, or homophobic remarks.

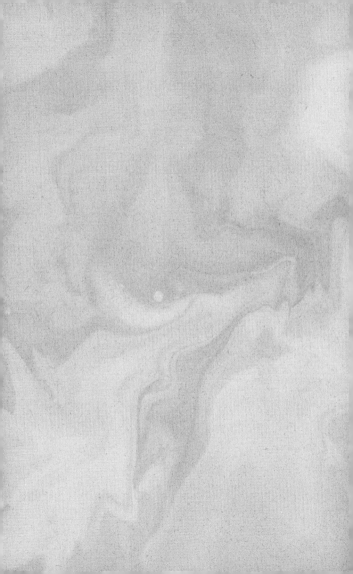

including those who have made racist, sexist, or homophobic remarks. Is cancel culture providing redemption? Or is it just attempting to pronounce final judgment on people who need grace and space to learn better ways of being?

DISCUSSION
QUESTIONS

1. What does it look like to disagree well? How do you want to respond when you disagree with someone?

2. How can we offer people redemption when they say or do offensive things?

3. Can you think of someone who deserves to be canceled? Why or why not? What should their cancellation look like?

4. Do you know anyone who has been canceled? What did that look like? Have you ever been afraid of getting canceled?

5. Define *justice* in your own words. What are some ways you can balance justice and mercy in the way you treat and talk about others?

6. What are some steps you can take to prepare to interact with people who disagree with you?

RECAP

- Cancel culture is complicated. It's an attempt to hold people accountable for harmful actions or words, but it gets applied to so many situations (including sexual harassment, racist language, unintentionally stupid or insensitive comments, and controversial ideas) that it's difficult to know if canceling someone (firing them, unfollowing them, etc.) provides true justice.

- Cancel culture is controversial. Some argue that it's a necessary tool to enforce social standards of appropriate speech. Others fear that it silences disagreement because espousing a controversial opinion could permanently damage someone's career or reputation.

- Navigating cancel culture is difficult, but scriptural principles can help us respond with wisdom and grace.

- Jesus' redemption is for everyone, even the people who deeply offend us. Being at peace with others doesn't mean glossing over differences of opinion or ignoring harmful ideas, but it does mean treating everyone respectfully, remembering that we are all God's image bearers.

- It's easy to think of people as either all good or all bad. In reality, each of us has a profound capacity to wound and a profound capacity to heal. We should remember how we want to be treated in moments of failure when we're tempted to cancel someone completely.

We should remember
how we want to be
treated in moments
of failure when we're
tempted to cancel
someone completely.

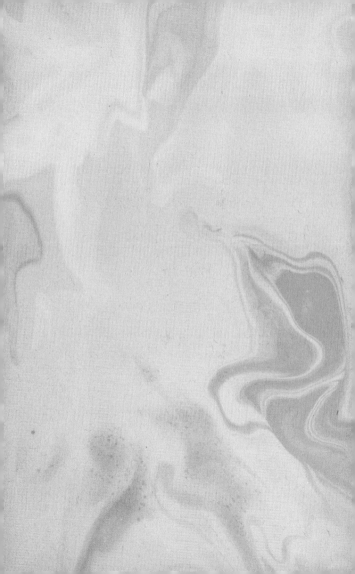

ADDITIONAL RESOURCES

1. Jonah Engel Bromwich, "Cancel Culture Part 1: Where It Came From," *The Daily* podcast, *New York Times*, https://www.nytimes.com/2020/08/10/podcasts/the-daily/cancel-culture.html

2. Jonah Engel Bromwich, "Cancel Culture, Part 2: A Case Study," *The Daily* podcast, *New York Times*, https://www.nytimes.com/2020/08/11/podcasts/the-daily/cancel-culture.html

3. Elliot Williams, "The 'I'm Not a Racist' Defense," CNN, https://www.cnn.com/2020/05/28/opinions/amy-cooper-apology-opinion-williams/index.html

4. "Podcast #34—Jonathan Haidt," *The Jordan B. Peterson Podcast*, https://www.jordanbpeterson.com/podcast/episode-34/

5. Heterodox Academy, https://heterodoxacademy.org/

6. Aja Romano, "Why We Can't Stop Fighting about Cancel Culture," Vox, https://www.vox.com/culture/2019/12/30/20879720/what-is-cancel-culture-explained-history-debate

7. Robert J. Zimmer, "Free Speech Is the Basis of a True Education," https://cpb-us-w2.wpmucdn.com/voices.uchicago.edu/dist/3/337/files/2019/01/Free-Speech-Is-the-Basis-of-a-True-Education-WSJ-1v5hqit.pdf

8. Sanam Yar and Jonah Engel Bromwich, "Tales from the Teenage Cancel Culture," *New York Times*, https://www.nytimes.com/2019/10/31/style/cancel-culture.html

9. Greg Lukianoff and Jonathan Haidt, *The Coddling of the American Mind: How Good Intentions and Bad Ideas Are Setting Up a Generation for Failure*

10. Sarah Hagi, "Cancel Culture Is Not Real—At Least Not in the Way People Think," *Time*, https://time.com/5735403/cancel-culture-is-not-real/

11. "We Can't Cancel Everyone," For Harriet, YouTube, https://www.youtube.com/watch?v=DOwWsvUeDF0&feature=youtu.be

12. John McWhorter, "Academics Are Really, Really Worried about Their Freedom," *Atlantic*, https://www.theatlantic.com

/ideas/archive/2020/09/academics-are
-really-really-worried-about-their
-freedom/615724/

13. Chimamanda Ngozi Adichie, "The
    Danger of a Single Story," TED, https://
    www.ted.com/talks/chimamanda_ngozi
    _adichie_the_danger_of_a_single_story

NOTES

1. Jonah E. Bromwich, "Why 'Cancel Culture' Is
   a Distraction," *New York Times*, August 14,
   2020, https://www.nytimes.com/2020/08/14
   /podcasts/daily-newsletter-cancel-culture
   -beirut-protest.html.

2. Aja Romano, "Why We Can't Stop Fighting about
   Cancel Culture," Vox, August 25, 2020, https://
   www.vox.com/culture/2019/12/30/20879720
   /what-is-cancel-culture-explained-history
   -debate.

3. Jan Ransom, "Amy Cooper Faces Charges
   after Calling Police on Black Bird-Watcher,"
   New York Times, July 6, 2020, https://www
   .nytimes.com/2020/07/06/nyregion/amy
   -cooper-false-report-charge.html.

4. Jonah Engel Bromwich, interview with
   Michael Barbaro, "Cancel Culture, Part 1:
   Where It Came From," *The Daily* (podcast),
   New York Times, August 10, 2020, https://
   www.nytimes.com/2020/08/10/podcasts/the
   -daily/cancel-culture.html.

5. Amir Vera, "Here Are Just Some of the People Who Were Canceled or Threatened with Cancellation in 2019," CNN, December 9, 2019, https://www.cnn.com/2019/12/08/us/2019-canceled-stories-trnd/index.html.

6. Sanam Yar and Jonah Engel Bromwich, "Tales from the Teenage Cancel Culture," *New York Times*, October 31, 2019, https://www.nytimes.com/2019/10/31/style/cancel-culture.html.

7. Romano, "Why We Can't Stop Fighting."

8. Bromwich, "Cancel Culture, Part 1."

9. Romano, "Why We Can't Stop Fighting."

10. Bromwich, "Cancel Culture, Part 1."

11. "A Letter on Justice and Open Debate," *Harper's Magazine*, July 7, 2020, https://harpers.org/a-letter-on-justice-and-open-debate/.

12. Jill K. Sanders, "Cancel Culture and Its Conflict with Criminal Justice Reform," Pappalardo & Pappalardo, LLP, July 17, 2020, https://pappalardolaw.com/2020/07/cancel-culture-conflicts-with-criminal-justice-system/.

13. Daniel Spielberger, "Everyone Is Getting Canceled in Quarantine. This Is Why We're Seeing More Stars in Hot Water Than Ever Before," Insider, May 31, 2020, https://www.insider.com/celebrity-fight-canceled-quarantine-why-were-seeing-feuds-doja-lana-2020-5.

14. Spielberger, "Everyone Is Getting Canceled."

15. Greg Lukianoff and Jonathan Haidt, *The Coddling of the American Mind: How Good Intentions and Bad Ideas Are Setting Up a Generation for Failure* (New York: Penguin Press, 2018), 29.

16. Geoffrey R. Stone, Statement on Principles of Free Inquiry, *University of Chicago News*, July 2012, https://cpb-us-w2.wpmucdn.com/voices.uchicago.edu/dist/3/337/files/2019/01/Statement-on-principles-of-free-inquiry-by-Prof.-Geoffrey-Stone-University-of-Chicago-News-1f1jp6l.pdf.

17. David Westmoreland and Connor Mccormick, "Embracing Flat Earth Science Denialism Can Help Us Overcome It," New Scientist, January 8, 2020, https://www.newscientist.com/article/mg24532642-900-embracing-flat

-earth-science-denialism-can-help-us
-overcome-it/.

18. Daryl Davis, "Why I, as a Black Man, Attend KKK Rallies," TEDxNaperville, video, 18:53, https://www.ted.com/talks/daryl_davis _why_i_as_a_black_man_attend_kkk _rallies?language=en.

19. Dan Allender, "Shame-Faced," Allender Center at the Seattle School, February 14, 2018, https://theallendercenter.org/2018/02/shame -faced/.

20. Maria Popova, "Fixed vs. Growth: The Two Basic Mindsets That Shape Our Lives," The Marginalian, accessed January 26, 2023, https://www.themarginalian.org/2014/01/29 /carol-dweck-mindset/.

21. Aleksandr Solzhenitsyn, quoted in Lukianoff and Haidt, *The Coddling of the American Mind*, 243.

22. Henri J. M. Nouwen, *Life of the Beloved: Spiritual Living in a Secular World* (New York: Crossroad, 1992), 59.

PARENT GUIDES TO SOCIAL MEDIA
BY AXIS

It's common to feel lost in your teen's world. Let these be your go-to guides on social media, how it affects your teen, and how to begin an ongoing conversation about faith that matters.

BUNDLE THESE 5 BOOKS AND SAVE

PARENT GUIDES TO FINDING TRUE IDENTITY
BY AXIS

When culture is constantly pulling teens away from Christian values, let these five parent guides spark an ongoing conversation about finding your true identity in Christ.

BUNDLE THESE 5 BOOKS AND SAVE